Effective Email

Also by Graham Jones

Abolish Public Speaking Fear
Fit To Manage
Future Planning
How to Do Business on the Internet
How to Manage Computers at Work
How to Publish a Newsletter
How to Sell Information Products
How to Start a Business from Home
How to Use the Internet
Naming a Website on the Internet
Personal Finance on the Internet
Promoting a Website on the Internet
Protecting Children on the Internet
The Business of Freelancing
Travel and Holidays on the Internet
Using Credit Cards on the Internet
Using the Internet

Effective Email

A guide to help you maximise your use of email and to ensure that your email doesn't control you!

By Graham Jones

First published in the UK in 2002. This edition published in 2012.

The moral right of Graham Jones has been asserted.

ISBN: 978-1-871550-49-8

Publisher's Note

Some of the quotations provided in this book have been given fictitious names in order to protect the identity of those who have made contributions. The fictitious names used are not meant to suggest that these are quotations provided by people who have the same or similar names. No connection to real people is implied or suggested.

You should seek proper advice on your own specific situation with regard to the implementation of email systems and policies.

About the author

Graham Jones, *B.Sc. (Hons), B.A. (Hons), Adv. Dip. Ed., MBPsS, M.Ed., M.Sc. FPSA,* is an Internet Psychologist who studies how people use the Internet. He helps businesses and organisations use the online world in better, more productive ways through consultancy, coaching, mentoring, workshops, masterclasses and speeches at conferences. Graham is the author of 28 books, including 12 about the Internet. He lives in Berkshire.

For more information see: www.grahamjones.co.uk

Acknowledgements

My thanks go to everyone who spoke to me about their experiences with email. Without their thoughts and suggestions this book would never have been written. Also, my thanks go to my son Elliot, for making me realise how exciting junk mail can be.

Graham Jones, Reading

About Effective Email

Can you organise an effective email system and be producing stunning messages all within an hour? The answer is a resounding "YES". This book sets out all you need to know to have a tip-top email system that is effective and efficient. In short, you'll get a blueprint to help you cope with every aspect of email. This book was written for people with neither the time nor the patience to trawl through acres of jargon, management-speak and page-filling waffle. *Effective Email* has been written in the belief that you can learn all you need to know quickly and without hassle. The aim is to distil the essential, practical advice you can use straight away.

Is this book for you?

Have you yet to venture into the world of email? Are you worried about the safety and security of email messages? If you already use email, do you get frustrated by the various options that are available to you? Do you receive lots of unwanted emails? Is your online privacy a worry to you? Do you find most emails boring? Do you find you are unable to 'speak' the email lingo? If you answer "YES" to any of these questions you'll find answers within this book.

However, if you want a manual that is full of the technical side of email — setting up specific programs or choosing from various options and commands — you won't find this book of much help. That's because this book is about using email effectively, so that your communications get results. This is not a book about using email programs; instead this book is dedicated to helping you maximise your effectiveness and efficiency with email.

How to use this book

The conventions used in this book are easy to follow.

> *Text like this is a quotation from people who use email and who provide an insight into efficiency and effectiveness.*

Text like this is an action point for you. You may need to consider carefully what is written in this format.

Text like this is a thought provoker.

Contents

Chapter 1

Why email is different

- ➤ Email is so boring
- ➤ How people use email at work
- ➤ How people use email at home
- ➤ When to use email

Email is so boring

> *"How wonderful it is to get letters from listeners. Here's one from John in Scunthorpe that is beautifully handwritten and makes its point so well. It's so nice to receive letters like this, rather than all those impersonal emails we get. So please, do write to us."*
> John Inverdale, speaking on BBC Radio Five Live

Every morning at 7am, when my son Elliot was around 18-months-old, he raced down the stairs on his nappy-padded bottom shouting 'post, post'. He scuttled towards the front door knocking everything down that might be in his way. He went head first onto the pile of letters on the doormat and threw them in the air, still shouting 'post, post'. The smile on his face spread from one ear to the next when he saw the letters. His huge grin stayed with him for ages, much longer than the time it took to jump up and down with excitement telling Daddy that the post had been delivered. We rushed headlong into the kitchen and as I sorted the letters I always managed to find some unwanted piece of junk mail that I could hand to him saying: 'Look Elliot, here's a letter for you.' At this point the excitement reached fever pitch as he sat down on the kitchen floor, ripped open the envelope and dispersed the contents all around the room. Still shouting 'post, post' he rushed around the house until he found Mummy so she could be shown the contents of his envelope.

Elliot was born in November 1999, well into the age of the Internet and email. Even though he loved the flashing of the computer screen and mucking about with the mouse and the keyboard, there was little to beat the excitement of receiving the morning post. Apart, that was, from hiding Daddy's car keys and then shrieking with hilarity!

Elliot is not alone in his excitement at receiving letters. We all love to open the mail, as we excitedly anticipate the contents. Who is it from? What will be inside? Is there money? Have I got the job?

Can you remember receiving your first love letter? Or do you recall the first letter you got offering you a job? Do you remember that first official letter you received?

Most of us can recall an emotional experience associated with receiving a letter or something in the mail. Letters have a sense of expectation associated with them. But they also have smells, colours and texture. You can smell the scent of a loved-one on their letters. You can feel the quality of the paper from that perfect old aunt. You are cheered up by the bright paper from your cousin. Have you ever associated anything like these thoughts with an email? Indeed, have you ever been excited to receive an email, reading it eagerly with your heart racing and your nerves on edge as you anticipate the final line? The chances are that you perceive email to be impersonal, lacking in any kind of emotion and, frankly, boring.

Find four different letters you have been sent and work out which elements of each letter trigger specific emotions. Try and find two or three factors in each piece of mail that lead to emotional reactions. By doing this you should arrive at some common themes that show how traditional letters make you react. These themes will help you ensure your future emails will be less personal. Knowing how post leads to emotional reactions will help you make your emails less boring.

How people use email at work

"Without email my working life would be a mess. I just simply have to use email to get everything organised on time. It helps me be much more efficient and I couldn't cope if I had to go back to posting letters."
Sally D, Marketing Manager, Software Company.

Most people under the age of 25 have never written a letter. That's the surprising statistic from a survey undertaken by MSN Hotmail, one of the leading email providers in the world. As we speed our way through the 21st Century, letter writing is becoming less common. It is so much easier to zap off an email and it is much more convenient. However, research conducted at the University of Illinois, Urbana-Champaign, USA, has found that as more and more people use email, their relationships are weakening. People who depend on email are maintaining less contact with people nearby to them. Instead, they are replacing frequent, close contact with few people, with infrequent contact with many more individuals, spread far and wide. In other words, they are spreading their human contact very thinly. It seems that 'email dependents' believe that the vast volume of emails they receive and generate is an indication of their popularity. It helps raise self-esteem — for a short time. Hence it needs to be repeated often to have any lasting impact. This means that people who survive by email need to generate thousands of emails each year to feel they are of any value.

Contrast this situation with someone who receives the occasional letter in the post. At first sight, a single letter may not be able to do much to raise self-worth. However, physical letters appear to have a much longer-lasting personal impact than emails. This means that people who don't use emails can have a greater sense of self-esteem with much less raw material. They don't need to generate so many letters to feel good.

Do you check your email on holiday?

A survey by Gartner has found that almost half of business people check their email while on holiday. So you are probably not alone. Checking email has become a comfort blanket for many people in business. In other words, email is increasingly being used to bolster personal values and self-belief, rather than to communicate.

> *"Email has become the corporate security blanket of this decade. If executives don't get their 22 emails per day, they actually miss them and begin to feel out of the loop."*
> Maurene Caplan Grey, research analyst at Gartner.

Further research by Gartner shows that only a quarter of all emails received at work require immediate attention. Added to that, it appears that one-third of the time people spend dealing with email is devoted to handling unnecessary messages. As if that were not enough, every employee of every company is now spending an hour a day replying to emails (many of them unnecessary). The result is that corporate efficiency and productivity is at its lowest level for decades and personal efficiency is at rock bottom. Emails are being used in business to make people think they are doing well, while constantly providing a smokescreen to real success.

From what you have read so far, consider your attitude to emails at work. Do you really need to receive all those emails you get? Do you really need to reply or comment on many of them? Do you need to send so many emails yourself? Are your emails really that necessary in the overall scheme of things?

How people use email at home

In the year 2000, some 50,000 people contacted The Samaritans via email for emotional support. That's almost twice the number of people who contacted the organisation by telephone. Since The Samaritans launched its email service, the number of users has doubled every year. This is a massive indication of one of the benefits of personal emailing. You can gain confidential, anonymous advice on anything from the simplest trivia, to sexual problems and severe, suicidal depression. Without the advent of email, many people may not have sought out such advice for fear of being identified. With email, anonymity has arrived.

"When I left school I wanted to study for a degree in technology, but went into a job instead. Now thanks to the Internet I have been able to study online. At first I thought I would need to see a tutor regularly, but I have found that email has come to the rescue. I can contact any of my tutors and get quick responses to my questions. This has really helped my studies."
Dave S, Online Undergraduate Student

When you don't want to be anonymous, email has other benefits. Online tutoring for students is a huge area of email usage; so too is personal coaching for things like confidence building. Fitness consultants use email to stimulate their clients and professional athletes even get inspiring emails from their coaches. These personal boosts via email are much more effective than a traditional letter as they have instant effects.

Email has also been responsible for reuniting friends and families that have lost touch over the years. It is so easy to lose touch, but with email you can quickly find someone again and re-establish your relationship.

> **Is there anyone you would love to get in contact with again, but don't know where to start? Looking for their email address may be a way to revive the relationship rather than just connecting on Facebook.**

On a personal front, email has huge benefits. It helps you achieve, it helps you maintain relationships and it helps you deal with difficulties in your life in a comfortable way. The way most people use email at home is positive and beneficial with a potentially huge emotional impact. The way most people use email at work, is largely negative, inefficient and a potentially vast economic impact on the business. Business email brings with it some increase in self-esteem, but at the cost of needing to work on even more emails. The comparison between the way email is used at work and at home shows that email has far more personal and emotional benefits than are evident at a first glance. Emails may not have the physical emotional triggers of the letter in the post, but they can be as powerful.

When to use email

"I receive about a dozen email messages each day that do not need an urgent reply. They could have been sent by post as there is no urgency to them."
Simon W, Product Manager, pharmaceutical manufacturer.

If all the statistics are to be believed, most people send emails without much thought. They simply rattle off a reply or send a message to someone because it is quick and easy to do. They appear to have little thought for the recipient. This is not the case for normal letters.

Most people consider carefully the letters they send. They think about what to say, often re-writing the material, and make choices about paper, envelope etc. With email, people don't appear to make such considerations. The result is, we are all receiving emails that are unnecessary and don't take us into account as the recipients.

How often do you simply reply to a message or send an email without stopping to think: 'is this the best method of communicating my message, to this individual'?

Email may be convenient and easy, but it can also make your reader less interested in what you have to say. Your emails can be deleted within a fraction of a second of reading the first few words. If your reader doesn't like what you are saying, doesn't believe it is for them or of interest, your message will be deleted straight away. That is so much more difficult with a letter, or a fax, or a phone call! Even so, emails are useful, providing they are used appropriately. This means emails are invaluable if:

➢ Your recipient needs to act straight away on your message.
➢ Your recipient has asked for your material by email.
➢ Your recipient prefers to receive emails rather than letters.
➢ Your recipient is away from their home or office and can't receive letters.
➢ Your recipient has impaired vision and can cope with emails much better than letters (emails can be converted to voice messages or can be viewed in very large text).
➢ Your recipient needs to receive additional material, such as data, that can be attached to your message but can't easily be sent by post.

As you can see, the decision whether to send an email is based on your recipient's needs, NOT your preferences. Communication works best when you take into account the requirements of your audience.

Look through your contact list and set about establishing the preferences of the people you know. Mark up your list according to who wants emails, which people prefer letters, who works away from their office frequently and so on. In this way you'll have a much more meaningful list of contacts that enables you to communicate more effectively.

In today's business world email is vastly over-used and is having a detrimental impact on many businesses. It is wasting time, reducing productivity and increasing costs. That's a real shame, because as people who use email in their personal life have discovered, email has huge benefits. The reason why email is different at work is because people perceive it as something that makes their life easier — yet in reality, it is making day-to-day working much more complex. You need to tame your email, get it under control and then it will be really effective. It is an extremely powerful form of communicating, but it is better if you are in charge of that power, rather than letting email control you. You can only really be in charge of email if you understand it and the impact it has.

TIPS:

- ➢ Make sure you know what method of communication suits your audience best.
- ➢ Only use an email if no other form of communication is more suitable.
- ➢ Email has a huge emotional impact on people, just like letters, so make your emails emotionally centred.
- ➢ Try to use emails at work in the same way as you do in personal life.

Chapter 2

Writing Great Emails

- ➢ How to write an email message
- ➢ How to keep messages short
- ➢ How to make emails interesting
- ➢ How to create impact

Do you often find that email messages sent to you have spelling mistakes, look untidy and have lots of abbreviations? Do you find that email messages are often quite long, quoting lots of text from previous messages? How would people react if you sent the same kind of message?

How to write an email message

When you receive email messages that make you react positively the person writing to you has almost certainly thought about YOU. They will have addressed their material directly to you, or will at least make you think they have with the choice of words they use. Good emails have been written from YOUR perspective, not the writer's.

> At this stage it would be a good idea if you could take a look through this book, quickly flicking through the pages. As you flick through, what is one of the most common words you see?

Good emails will feel as though they are having a conversation with you. You will almost 'hear' the person talking to you. Indeed, as you flicked through this book, you should have noticed that a very common word is 'you'. You should almost feel as though I am talking directly to you, though the chances are we have never met and don't know each other. You see how being direct and conversational has such a dramatic impact on you?

You will be able to see which emails you have previously received that have had the most impact by going through a dozen or so and checking the wording. Those that are personal, that use the word 'you' and appear to be written from your perspective are most likely to be the ones you found most appealing. You can check this now by going through some of the emails you have received.

The first step in making your emails personal is to address the person by name – as you would in a letter. Instead of starting off your email with your text, start with 'Dear (name)', just as you would with a letter. The recipient will feel you are addressing them directly – already you will have had a positive emotional impact on your reader. Few people who send emails use this approach. Instead, they just start with the text, or the background to their material. From the recipient's perspective such emails could have been sent to anyone.

The next key step is to adopt a conversational style. Avoid clichés and 'business-speak'. Just write your text in much the same way as you would say it if the person were in front of you.

> *"One of my bosses sends emails that sound as though he is right next to you chatting away. Another senior director sends emails that are full of formal, business language. He thinks he is better at sending emails, but we don't have the heart to tell him that the informal messages from my boss have far more of an impact on us."*
> Alan H, Technical support manager, Telecoms Company.

Get straight to the point. Don't waste your time with lots of pre-amble. One of the reasons why people like email is because of its speed. Increasing the amount of time people need to take to read your emails means that you are making them react negatively to what you have to say. Just dive straight in — just as you would in a conversation.

Another important aspect of being conversational is using the word 'you' frequently. Try to get this somewhere in your first sentence. If you find your emails are using the words 'I' or 'me' quite a bit, try to re-write them, this time from the recipient's viewpoint. That will force you to use the words 'you' and 'your' more frequently. Try to imagine you are the person receiving the email. This will help you focus your mind on the way to write your text.

How often do you think about the person to whom you are writing? When it's personal do you have a picture of them in your mind?

Having a picture of the person you are writing to in your mind is really helpful as it makes you be much more direct. As I write this, I have a picture of YOU in my mind. Of course it isn't really YOU, but it is someone. I can actually see, in my mind's eye, someone sitting down reading this book. It's so much easier to be direct when you have such a vision. When you write your emails in a detached way, your reader will also be detached from what you are saying. As a result you email will have far less impact.

> *"I write a column for a women's magazine and each month I sit down to write it I have a picture in my mind of Maggie. She is 40, has two children aged 10 and 13 and lives in Coventry. She wears clothes from Debenhams and shops at Tesco. She drives a blue Renault Scenic and works in a travel agency. It might be a stereotype, but it means I know who I am writing for; otherwise my column would not hit the target for the magazine."*
> Annie S, magazine columnist

How to keep messages short
Sometimes email messages can get quite long, especially when you quote much of the material that has been sent in previous emails. Also,

emails often get long if you have a lot to say or you need to give a comprehensive overview of a particular business situation.

Which emails do you respond to quickly and with a positive frame of mind — the short ones or the lengthy, in-depth emails?

> Sort through all your emails and letters and faxes and sort them into two distinct kinds – the short ones and the long ones. Now, look through each pile and find the ones that you really liked and responded well to.

Most people tend to find that the letters and emails they received that are short are the ones they responded to most positively and had the best feelings about. Long letters do get a positive response — however, almost invariably, long communications are only given a positive rating if we have a very close and warm relationship with the person who has written to us. We rarely feel positive towards acquaintances and people we do not know who send us long letters or emails. This has important implications for people using email in business. A sizeable proportion of your emails at work are going to be sent to people you do not know or have only the slimmest of relationships with. Hence anything other than a short email is likely to lead towards a negative feeling in your reader. Play safe; keep it short!

This is all very well in theory, of course, but in practice, particularly at work, you need to include a lot of material. The answer is to treat the email as though it were a covering letter. Then attach the main text as a separate word processor document. All email programs can attach files to them, yet vast numbers of emails are sent without using this facility. The advantage of putting your main material in an attachment is that your recipient immediately views your message in a positive light because it is short and to the point. You should summarise the content of the attachment in a sentence or two — in that way your reader can gain all they need to know, without having to open the attached file. However, if they need more depth you have provided it for them.

"One of the techniques we use in the office for reports is to produce a one-page 'Executive Briefing'. This is a summary of the report on just one side of paper, even though the main document can be up to 100 pages long. I just wish people would follow the same principle with their emails. They could summarise what they needed to say in a few lines and attach the detail in a longer document in case I want to read it. Instead, they send out these great long emails and I have to wade through them to get to the point."
Natalie B, Administration Manager, local authority

One technique you can use for shortening your email is to write the main message in your word processing software, with all the detail you need. Then take a break, do something else and later on, read through your text. Now try to summarise it in a few sentences – that summary should be the main part of your email. Trying to summarise something you have just written is difficult as all the detail will still be in your mind. That's why taking a break can help you as you leave your mind uncluttered and make summary writing much easier. Your summary email, together with the word processor document as an attachment is much more likely to please your recipient. This means there is considerable value in taking time to construct your email properly, rather than just dashing something off.

Another way in which you can be sure of keeping emails short is to avoid 'quoting' vast amounts of previous emails. One of the benefits of the 'reply' button on most email programs is that you can quote the previous email. In this way the recipient can easily see what you are responding to. However, since many emails go back and forth between various people, the message can quickly become very long indeed — even though most of it is material from previous messages. The answer to solving this is to only quote what you need to send someone in order to make your reply understandable. By all means, press the 'reply' button to quote the original email, but then go through the quoted text and delete everything that is irrelevant to what you are going to write about. Doing so is seeing the message from your reader's viewpoint — they don't want to wade through the original text (their own!) just to see which point you are commenting on. It is much easier from their viewpoint if your reply is clear. In other words, only use selective quoting — not wholesale quoting of emails as is the most common practice.

Do you find you have to scroll down through emails to previously written text, just to find out what the author is responding to? Frustrating isn't it?

An additional reason why some emails are so long is because the author is trying to cover various topics. They are almost 'brain dumping' everything they can think of that is important or relevant to the reader. Meanwhile, the poor recipient has to work their way through this mess to try and find out what is important. Good communication, particularly to people we don't know, is focused communication. That means, in essence, that each email should be about one topic and one topic only. A hint to this is given in the email software itself where you have to type a 'subject' for your email.

"There is one person in our office who I just can't cope with when it comes to emails. Each day he fires off an email at the end of the day to a great long list of people. The message is about a stack of different things, only a couple of which are probably relevant to me. But because his message is about so much, his subject line says something inane like 'Various'. That makes me mad!"
Andy W, Software Engineer, Web Development Company

If your emails are about more than one subject – stop! Each email should only be about one subject. Your recipient will react far more positively if you sent four separate short emails about four subjects than trying to cram all the material into one, inevitably longer message. Also, when these separate messages get replied to, the quoted material is shorter. Hence, think always, one message — one email.

How to make emails interesting

You will have already noticed that one of the main ways to make your emails interesting is to keep them short and conversational. But there are many more things you can do to help make your emails interesting. For a start, look at the words you use and the way you write things. Usually, most conversational writing is full of passion, enthusiasm and excitement. The language of business, however, is flat, dull and monotone.

Which kind of written material do you prefer to read – something that is exciting and passionate about its subject, or something that is dull and lifeless?

Email messages that convey enthusiasm and that appear full of vigour are much more interesting than those which are dull, cliché-ridden and virtually comatose. Even if you are not that excited about the latest developments in your business world, your emails can convey positive feelings if you choose your words carefully. So, take time to construct your emails. Think about the words you are using and if necessary, use a thesaurus to find synonyms that will add flavour and enthusiasm to what you are saying. The extra minute or two taken to write emails that appear to be alive is time well-spent if you get a positive reaction from your reader. If you send something that's dull and inert, you are not likely to achieve the results you want; hence your message will be wasted. A little extra time to bring alive what you are saying will pay huge dividends.

> Check out your email program's facilities. Some include the ability to incorporate a thesaurus. Others can be enhanced with dictionary facilities. It's a good idea to make sure you use the writing capabilities of your email software to the full.

One way of making sure your emails are seen as enthusiastic and full of life is to write from the heart. Try to avoid being business-like; instead try to write the way you FEEL about something, rather than what you think. Inject more of the real YOU into your messages and less of the professional business person you are trying to be! Studies across businesses throughout the world show that when people try to write things in a business-like manner, they actually reduce the chances of someone understanding what they have said. People who communicate in business on a personal level are the ones who have the greatest impact.

One of the key reasons why certain letters stand out in your mind is because they are personal — love letters, for instance. The person writing to you not only addressed you personally, but also spoke personally, talking about the way they felt. Yet, when it comes to business, many people abandon such a warm and passionate way of talking and become cold and stilted, because they think it is professional. It may well seem to be professional, but it is less effective. Your emails will be interesting if they are written with feeling and not written with detachment. When you write with feeling you will inevitable use language that is alive and colourful.

> Take any email message or letter you have received
> recently and to which you have sent a reply. Look at the
> message you received and write down what you FELT
> about what you were sent. What was your initial reaction?
> What was your 'gut feeling'? Now compare what you
> have just written down to the reply you sent. Which one
> has the most colourful and interesting language? The
> chances are that what you have just written is more
> passionate than your original reply.

Another useful way of making your emails interesting is to write them
so that you start to form pictures in the mind of your recipient. Be
descriptive, use words like 'imagine', or phrases like 'picture the
scene'. Give examples that highlight what you are saying. When you
are descriptive and allow your reader to form mental pictures you have
so much more impact. Much of our memory is pictorial – indeed some
psychologists argue that we think and remember almost entirely on a
visual basis. Hence, if you help your reader construct pictures around
what you are saying your material is seen as much more interesting –
plus it becomes more memorable. So instead of saying things like:

*"You will notice that the attached report highlights the importance of
the Internet in our future sales programme."*

Say something like:

*"If you look through the report I've attached you'll notice that in the
year ahead I'm sure we'll gain from a sharp increase in people sitting
at home in the evening, logging onto our Internet site, and buying
directly from us."*

This conveys the same overall message, but in a much more interesting
and pictorial way.

How to create impact

> Sort through your emails or letters and find ones that are
> not from people you know well. Now divide these into
> those that had a real impact on you and 'the rest'. Take a
> look at the ones that had an impact. What common
> features do they have?

Emails that have an impact are either immensely personal or have some
other features that made you sit up and take notice. These factors are
additional to the writing style and the shortness of the message. One
key element often neglected in email is colour. We see in colour, our
entire world is in colour and then we communicate in black and white
emails. How boring! Email programs can add colour and brighten up
your text no-end. Many people avoid using colour because they cannot
be sure that the colour will 'come through' to the recipient. In the old
days of email messaging, this was true. The computers around the
world that made up the email systems would often not be able to
interpret the colour coding and so it was deleted. Things have moved
on apace, though. 'Rich Text' and HTML emails allow you to send
emails that include colour, bold and italic text and other stylistic
features. Sending emails in this way allows you to create greater
impact. True, some systems delete all such enhancing features from
incoming emails, but the majority do not. So it's probably not a good
idea to send 'plain text' emails, just because a minority of computers
won't handle the enhanced emails properly.

"I've noticed that quite a few emails these days look like mini web pages. They are bright and colourful and catch your attention. They are so much more interesting than the boring ones I get from head office."
Jamie H, Sales Executive, electronics retailer

Most email programs can now send messages in what is known as HTML format. This is the computer coding language that is used to construct web pages (Hyper Text Mark-up Language). You don't have to know how to use this code as many programs exist to help you produce messages that can incorporate graphics, dynamic elements and interactive components. Providing you make your email messages personal and short, you can dramatically enhance their impact by making them into mini web pages by sending them in HTML format.

Find out how your email message program goes about constructing and sending messages in HTML format. Either look in the manual or the online help facility, or go to the program publisher's web site. If you can easily construct HTML format messages you can enhance your emails significantly.

If you can't cope with HTML, or your program does not support it, you can still create additional impact — and you can even do this with plain text messages! Add headings and sub headings. Use rows of stars to break things up so they stand out. With a few of these headings and breaks you can provide a series of signposts to help your reader find their way through a message. Even in very short messages, a heading or two can help. They are not a lot different to the reference line you often get at the start of a traditional letter. They help the reader understand more clearly what the following text is about.

> **How do you react to the funny squiggles you often see in email messages? What do you think when people end their message with ;-) ? Do you really know what this means?**

Something that people try to use to convey their message is called an 'emoticon'. These little squiggles are supposedly ways of putting emotion across in your email. In the YOU box above, the emoticon is supposedly someone winking at you. To see this more clearly, turn the page through 90 degrees to the right. Now you can see the eyes, the nose and the smiling mouth.

Emoticons were invented prior to the availability of Rich Text and HTML email systems. They are supposed to convey faces and can be drawn with keyboard textual items, such as colons and brackets. Emoticons were also invented by people in business and academia – areas where emotion and passion in language have almost been obliterated by the culture within which these people work. It is perfectly possible to convey your emotions in the words you use. You don't need to use emoticons, if you write your email properly. The only problem is that this will take you longer. Emoticons are the shorthand, allowing you to convey your feelings instantly. The problem is this speed benefit is for YOU and not for the recipient. Most people who receive emoticons spend time trying to work out what on earth the squiggle means. Is it a typing mistake? Is it conveying what you really think it is? The danger of emoticons is that your recipient wastes time trying to work out what it means AND can interpret it differently to your intention. From your recipient's perspective emoticons are almost entirely negative. It's quite simple to convey your feelings and emotions accurately in your text. The extra time you take to write in this way will pay huge dividends as you will be effective in your communications. Just think of the time you would have to spend unravelling the problems if your recipient misunderstood your intentions. With good writing and with Rich Text or HTML emails, you just don't need emoticons.

"One of the girls in my office put a little sign after her name on each email she sent me. I thought it showed a face blowing a kiss and I thought she fancied me. So I asked her out. I was really embarrassed to find out she was living with a bloke and they were getting married later this year. It turned out the sign was on all the emails she sent to everyone and it only meant 'cheerio'."
Patrick J, Accountant, consultancy firm

Another aspect about emoticons is the fact that they can make emails look untidy. Some people may even think they are mistakes. Because many people rattle off emails quickly and with little thought, spelling mistakes and grammatical errors are frequent. Most email programs can check your email messages before you send them, but few default to this option. So it's a good idea to change the options on your email system so that messages are checked before you send them. That way, your recipient will not think you are sloppy and untidy — as is conveyed if you have spelling mistakes and other errors in your text.

What do you think when people send you emails with spelling errors and basic mistakes in them? Do you approach these messages more positively or more negatively?

TIPS:

> ➤ Put yourself in the position of the recipient and write from their viewpoint.
> ➤ Write personally, using words like 'you' and 'your' frequently.
> ➤ Only write on one subject in each email; if you need to cover more subjects separate them into distinct messages.
> ➤ Write a meaningful subject line for each email.
> ➤ Use colourful and enthusiastic language that enlivens each email.
> ➤ Use examples and paint word pictures wherever possible.
> ➤ Enhance your messages with colour, headings and so on.
> ➤ Try not to use emoticons as they can confuse.
> ➤ Check your emails for spelling mistakes before you send them!

Chapter 3

Receiving emails you want

- ➢ Sorting out the junk
- ➢ Avoiding mailing lists
- ➢ Filtering out important email
- ➢ Getting better replies

Sorting out the junk

If you thought the amount of junk mail you receive through your letterbox each day was bad enough, just wait — you ain't seen nothin' yet! Junk email is a huge and growing industry that will provide vast amounts of messages that will clog up your inbox. On average, everyone who has an email service receives 180 messages each day. Of course, many people receive only an occasional message from family or friends, so some people must be receiving enormous numbers of emails.

> *"I have now stopped counting the number of email messages I get. In fact I had to appoint a new assistant whose sole job is to sort through the emails I was receiving each day, just to prioritise them! He told me last week that the average daily inbox amounted to 275 messages. They all have to be read, sorted, many need replies and some need me to act. Happily, my assistant Simon only forwards about half a dozen emails a day that really need my attention."*
> Fiona R, European Marketing Director

Researchers are suggesting that based on the current growth in 'direct email' (junk to you and me!) we can expect 400 billion such messages to be sent each year. That will be 500 for every individual who has email, or around ten each week per person. While that may not seem much, the direct email companies don't have every email address, so some people can expect large amounts of unsolicited email messages.

The reason why companies want to do this is obvious. It's much cheaper than traditional direct mail. There are no printing costs, for a start and distribution is the price of a local phone call. Direct email is therefore virtually free for companies doing it. In addition, the returns are much greater than traditional direct mail. On average, only one person in every 100 replies to junk mail — it is 99% ineffective! In contrast, direct email has a huge response rate of between 11% and 35%. Properly targeted, direct email can get a response from one in three potential customers, compared with one in a hundred for traditional junk mail. Add to this the low costs and the profitability of direct email is beyond the wildest dreams of most businesses. You can therefore expect all the predictions about direct email to be wrong – the business case for it is overwhelming and companies around the world will be taking this up in vast numbers. Hence you can expect much, much more than 90 unsolicited emails a week.

Do you get annoyed with the junk mail which lands on your doormat a couple of times a week? How do you think you would react if you were to receive dozens of unsolicited emails? Have you considered how you may organise your email system to prevent unwanted emails?

Worse still, is the problem of 'spam'. This is the name given to untargeted, unsolicited email sent out by the truck load! The early Internet users adopted this name in recognition of the repeated emails that were being sent unsolicited – the word 'spam' is repeated endlessly in a Monty Python sketch. (Spam is actually a registered trade mark of the Hormel Corporation, which manufactures the processed meat product of the same name.) 'Spamming' – the act of sending out vast volumes of email to large address lists – is frowned upon by serious users of the Internet.

However, there are sufficient people who perform spamming to annoy you! Even so, spamming must work and produce profitable results otherwise companies would not do it. For most of us though, the receipt of 'spam' is a real hindrance.

> Sort through your list of received emails and find any from people you don't know and are unable to identify. Check through them and make sure they are really unwanted. Then copy their email addresses into plain text file. This will be the start of your 'junk' list and will be the first set of people you can block from sending material to you in the future.

Most email programs allow you to block unwanted messages, by adding the address of the sender to a 'junk list'. You will need to have a list of email addresses you do not want to hear from and when you get new unsolicited messages, you can add the addresses of the sender to your list. If your email program does not have such an option you can download add-ons from various web sites.

Every time you get junk mail, add it to your list and you will never hear from the sender again as the address will be blocked by your program. Also, don't reply to senders of unsolicited emails — especially to ask to be deleted from their mailing list. Spammers use programs that can generate guesswork email addresses. By replying, you are confirming your real email address and they can put you on their proper list. If you don't reply, they probably won't bother you again if they have just guessed your address.

Avoiding mailing lists

Do you dutifully fill in forms with all your details correctly? When applying for information online do you provide all the information you are asked for? If so, your data could be added to a mailing list.

Within Europe and the United States, there are strict controls over the addition of your personal information to a database. The Data Protection Acts in the UK and their associated European legislation means that no company or individual is allowed to maintain information about you in any kind of database unless they have paid a registration fee to do so and explained prior to registration exactly what they intend doing with your data. Even once they have done this they still cannot use your data without your express permission. The rules are somewhat different for American companies taking data from Europe, but the central tenet remains — your details are YOURS and only you can decide what people do with them.

However, there are two problems with the way your information is dealt with. Firstly, you have to tick a box or sign something to explain what permissions you are giving. Many companies put this in the small print and hence can easily sign away your rights to privacy without realising it. Secondly, many mailing lists are run by companies not covered by the European and American legislation as they are based in other parts of the world. Hence in the global world of email, data protection laws offer only limited safeguards.

"I found I was receiving emails almost every week from a company in some remote island who I had never heard of. I had no idea how they got my email address or why they even thought I would be interested in their products, which seemed like 'get rich quick' schemes to me. In the end I had to change my email address to avoid them."
Ellen H, mother and homemaker.

Because you cannot guarantee your email address will be kept private, you should take care with who you give it to. Firstly, unless you want a reply from the person or web site who demands your email address, give a false one! That way you won't hear from them again. However, this will only really work if you give a false email address via the web, the newsgroups or via phone or fax. If you use your email program to send a false address, your real email address is sent as well!

The second technique you can use is to have two email addresses. The first one is your real one that you give only to trusted people. The second is your 'public' email address that you give to those people you don't want to hear from. The difference is that you don't access your public email address, except on an occasional basis to see if there is anything of interest amongst the hundreds of messages. If you find one or two, you can then just delete the rest without reading them. You can get second email addresses that you only access occasionally from a host of different suppliers on the Internet. Many people use 'web mail' providers like Gmail, GMX, Hotmail, Yahoo! Mail and Zoho Mail to act as their second email address. You can also get email services, such as from www.mail.com, to provide you with an additional email address that forwards email to your main address, having filtered out the junk!

Get yourself a second email address that you use for non-trusted organisations and individuals. You can get these secondary email addresses instantly online via a range of web sites. If you get one, you'll be able to manage and avoid vast amounts of unwanted email.

Some email programs, such as Outlook or Thunderbird, allow you to create separate 'identities' so that you can manage your email in a similar fashion, without having to set up accounts with different email suppliers.

Filtering out important mail

One of the reasons why you want to use email is that you can receive messages that you need to act on quickly. Also, you'll want to receive messages and information that would be difficult to receive in another way. If you start to view email negatively because of the vast amount of junk you receive, you won't benefit from the positive aspects. Hence, you need to find a way of making sure that the emails you really want to receive are highlighted in advance. In that way you can concentrate on them, leaving the other — less important — messages until you get more time. However, how do you sort out the important emails before you have even read them? Thankfully almost every email program provides a method of filtering your email and sorting out the 'really important' from the 'not so important', according to a set of rules you establish.

Are there people who you receive email from that you really need to look at straight away? They may be important clients, your boss, or your partner — whoever it may be, there are probably some people who send you emails who deserve greater attention than others. Draw up your list of priority email addresses and save this as a plain text file. You will be able to use this file in the filtering functions that email programs provide.

"One of the most useful parts of my email system is the function that lets me categorise email addresses as to how important they are to me. Then, when email comes in it is presented in the right order for me, with the most important email at the top. The program does half my work for me, automatically. I just wish there was something similar for the morning post!"
Alan D, freelance journalist

If you establish filters based on email addresses you can then sort your incoming mail according to which of those addresses are the most or least important to you. In this way, your incoming email is always sorted in priority. Just start at the top and work down the list. Not every email program will allow you to do this, but all programs will allow you to filter the most wanted from the least wanted emails. In addition many email programs can learn and apply rules automatically.

Do you find that you waste time reading through emails that look important, but were really only of marginal relevance to you? Would it have been more efficient to have ignored these emails and look at a bunch of them when you had a gap in your schedule?

Another way in which you can sort your emails is to set up a range of different 'inboxes'. Email programs do allow you to have more than one 'inbox' – the directory or folder that stores your incoming email. It is a simple procedure to set up different inboxes for different categories of mail. For instance, you might want one inbox for internal office emails, another for personal emails and yet another for emails from customers. Or you might want an inbox for each of your main contacts. Or you could have different inboxes for each country that you deal with. The categories you set up for your inboxes will be specific to your needs as you can set them up yourself based on your own criteria. Most email programs will then pre-sort the incoming emails into the relevant inboxes for you. In this way you can glance down the list of inboxes, see which ones have mail and act on those which are most important to you.

Why not devise a list of inbox categories that you would like to use? If you sort your mail according to your own requirements, it will be much easier to administer the system. Unsorted email takes a long time to work through, so it is much better if you have it sorted in advance in the way you want to use it.

If you use separate inboxes, together with filtering based on individual email addresses you will have a highly sophisticated email system that you can easily manage. If you also block spam and junk emails, you will be able to whiz through your incoming messages with ease. However, that assumes that everyone who sends you a message is producing easy-to-read messages, that are short, interesting and attention grabbing!

Getting better replies

The email you receive is an indication of the kind of messages you send. If your incoming email is lengthy, uninteresting and not very stimulating there is a fair chance people are replying to you in the way you approached them! Hence, if you take the time to make your emails vibrant and colourful, the chances are that you will get positive and appealing responses. In other words, if you send out good email messages, you increase the likelihood of receiving great replies that are easy to deal with.

> *"Whenever my assistant sends me an email it is always short, to the point and interesting. It makes me reply more positively and the reply is always easy to do. But when my boss sends me his long rambling emails I find it hard to reply, I don't really want to and then I find I have to write great long screeds of text just to answer his points. I just wish he'd take a tip from Sally."*
> Adam J, Bank Manager.

If you send out long rambling emails, you will, in all likelihood, get long boring replies back. This will make your email administration much more difficult. So the first step in ensuring great replies is to provide short, interesting emails, as suggested in Chapter 2: Writing Great Emails.

The next step is to make it easy for people to reply. Ask them direct questions and leave space for them to insert their replies. Also, some email programs allow you to add buttons for answering questions 'yes' or 'no'. If your program supports them, it is a good idea to use them as people can quickly reply — plus you can rapidly check the response.

Check out the various feature enhancements of your email program so you can see which elements will help you construct messages that will generate simple replies.

Another way of enhancing the replies you get is to construct an HTML-based email message that generates much of the reply when people click on a 'reply' button. For instance, it can automatically insert the subject line that makes sense to YOU; or it can insert the entire reply text, allowing the sender just to add their name or a PS. The technology involved in generating such automated replies may well require the assistance of expert programmers. However, if you work in a business where you are likely to receive many replies from your recipients, such an automated reply system using HTML will save hours of working sorting through the incoming messages.

One final problem with controlling your inbox relates to the way you send out messages to large groups of people. It is tempting to put everyone's address in the 'To:' box. However, this means you are showing everyone the addresses of each recipient. If any of these recipients forwards the message, they will send every email address, including your own to other people. This is how large numbers of email addresses get distributed across the world.

To make sure you don't distribute a 'mailing list' like this, put all the addresses you want to reach in the 'Bcc:' box. This stands for 'blind carbon copy' and means the email is sent to everyone you want it to reach, but the addresses are not distributed. You will need to put at least one address in the 'To:' box, so put your own. If you put the whole list of addresses in the 'To:' box, you will not only contribute to the lists of spammers, but you will start to get 'flamed'. This is the term given to people sending you angry emails — many people who you listed in the 'To:' box will flame you because they will be upset you have distributed their email address to everyone on the list, without their permission. Hence, if you don't use the 'Bcc:' box, you'll end up with a vastly inflated inbox. Also, in the UK, unless you have specifically registered such distribution of email addresses under the Data Protection Act (1998), you will have committed an offence!

Use a signature

One reason why some people don't get the replies they want, where they want them or in the way they want is because they don't let anyone know how to get in touch with them. Sometimes, it would be better to respond to your email with a phone call. On other occasions it might be more appropriate to write a letter. Equally, you might want people to respond to your 'public' email address, rather than your private one. To ensure that all this happens you need to include all your contact information at the end of each email and tell people how you want to get a reply – do you want them to email you back or call you.

At first sight this may sound time consuming, but all email programs allow you to add a 'signature' that you keep in a separate text file. These signatures can include all the details you want and you can have different signatures for different purposes. If you set up a range of signatures, you will ensure that people can reply to you in the most appropriate manner as they'll have the information they need. Simply putting your name at the end of your email is not very helpful, so people will only be able to reply to the email address contained in the 'header' of the email – which may be your private address.

You can use a variety of signatures to suit all kinds of situations and a great system to make this easy is called WiseStamp from www.wisestamp.com.

TIPS:

> ➢ Only release your email address to people you trust.
> ➢ Get a second email address that becomes your 'public' address.
> ➢ Check you are not allowing your email address to be passed on to others when filling in forms online. Data protection rules will allow you to make sure this doesn't happen, but it will be in the web site's small print — so check it.
> ➢ Set up blocks for email addresses that are the source of junk email.
> ➢ Set up filters to help you prioritise your important incoming email messages.
> ➢ Organise your incoming email into a variety of different inboxes, categorised according to your needs.
> ➢ Ensure you get good replies by constructing emails that are easy to reply to.
> ➢ Use HTML emails to enable automated replies, thus reducing your administration time in handling incoming messages.
> ➢ Be sure to use the 'Bcc:' box when sending out mass emails to avoid dozens of angry emails from people who didn't want you to distribute their address.
> ➢ Use a signature to ensure people can respond to you in the best way.

Chapter 4

Establishing a safe system

- ➤ Protecting your inbox
- ➤ How to avoid email viruses
- ➤ Keeping messages secret
- ➤ Using digital 'IDs'

Protecting your inbox

Your message inbox is extremely valuable. It contains all of the important mail you have received as well as the addresses of everyone who has contacted you. In addition, your inbox will include the addresses of people who have sent you mail who you would rather not hear from again. If you lose your inbox or it becomes damaged in any way, you will lose important data. This will include the email addresses of people you have yet to put into your address book as well as the addresses of people you have not added to your filters, but want to. In addition, any attachments you have been sent will also be lost if your inbox is harmed in any way. Hence protecting your inbox from damage is essential to anyone using email.

Do you make regular backups of your computer disks? How often do you make copies of important files? Can you locate important backup files instantly?

We all know how important it is to backup our computer data files, yet most people do not perform backups. According to one study only one computer in every five is properly backed up. Without maintaining copies of your essential files in your email system, you will risk losing valuable data. Most firms that lose their essential files are not in business one year later — even if they have managed to recover the lost material to some extent. For home users of computers, loss of data can be frustrating and time consuming to replace. In many cases, because backing up was not performed properly, lost data is virtually irrecoverable. Specialist companies do exist that can locate as much of the lost information as possible — but it is expensive. Recovery will cost from £100 to more than £300 to recover! Hence, no matter whether you are using email for business or pleasure, backing up your inbox is vital. To do this you should follow the ABC of backing up:

> - Activate a backup policy.
> - Backup every day.
> - Check your backup files are working.

If you don't have a backup program and know how to use it, get one now! Also, make sure you have some other medium for your backup other than your original disk. Consider tapes, external drives and even online storage at specialist Internet backup sites such as a cloud computing site like Google Drive or Backupify.

> *"A month or so ago, my PC crashed after we had a power cut. It destroyed my hard drive and the only way my dealer could get me going again was to reformat the drive and re-install Windows. That meant all my data was erased and I had to reconstruct most of it. It took about two weeks just to get back to something approaching normal, but I've lost hundreds of email addresses and loads of useful files that have taken years to accumulate. I backup every day now!"*
> Chris B, local councillor.

Your email system will probably not accumulate all the necessary files in one place. Most email programs use a variety of different folders in which to place the various bits of data it uses. Hence if you only backup the main folder that contains your inbox, you could easily miss out some important data. By far the best method of ensuring you have a proper, functioning backup is to store copies of EVERY file on your PC. Also, check your backups work by restoring some files to your hard disk and trying to open them. Many backup strategies fail because people do not test their backup files. When you really need them it's too late to discover they don't work!

A further way to protect your inbox is to prune it each week. This means deleting all the unnecessary files, adding email addresses to your address book if necessary and updating your filters. As your inbox grows, you increase the likelihood of errors; keeping it compact and tidy will minimise the risk of damage. It will also mean that your administration of email is eased as your filters will be up-to-date. Even if you use webmail you should do this.

How to avoid email viruses

The most common cause of damage to email systems is some kind of virus that spreads throughout the world in hours. Prior to the widespread use of email, computer viruses were spread by swapping floppy disks between computers. This meant the number of viruses was pretty low and also it took time for them to spread. That allowed people to be alerted to the viruses and put in place defence mechanisms. Nowadays, with the extensive use of email, someone who invents a virus can have it infect PCs around the world in less than a day. There are tens of thousands of known viruses that affect computers and many of them are specifically spread via email. Not only can they damage your email system, they can corrupt your entire computer. It is therefore essential that everyone who uses email has up-to-date anti-virus protection in place.

> *"Our business has just five PCs and we installed an anti-virus program. What I didn't realise was that we needed to update this program regularly. Six months after buying it we were infected by a virus sent to us in an email message. It was a nightmare and putting it right wasted three days of work, costing us thousands."*
> Nick B, Managing Director, accountancy firm

Buy an anti-virus program suitable for your computer, making sure it can be automatically updated via the

> Internet. This is the only way you can be sure your
> computer is constantly protected.

Your anti-virus program needs to be constantly updated if it is to be effective. Most of the main programs, such as those from Norton, McAfee or Kaspersky, can be updated automatically via the Internet. Also, you will need to make sure that the program can scrutinize incoming emails for viruses — you need to check that the program can monitor what is known as a 'POP3' connection. 'POP3' is the jargon for the email system that delivers your messages to you. Those anti-virus programs that can integrate with your POP3 system will be able to block viruses before they get to your machine. If you use IMAP instead of POP3 make sure your antivirus can cope with it.

Many Internet Service Providers (ISPs) provide monitoring of their email systems to prevent viruses from spreading. You can add a further layer of protection by enabling this system, if your ISP provides it. You will probably have to pay an additional annual fee, but the cost is minimal in comparison with the losses you would incur if infected with a virus.

Have you prepared for virus attacks on your email system? Have you also thought about how you would guard yourself against new viruses that anti-virus software cannot yet detect?

The programmers who produce anti-virus software are working hard to update their products and provide as rapid a service as they can. However, if a new virus is sent to your email system, there is a chance that even if you have the latest update, your computer could be damaged. For this reason you need some additional protection that blocks anything that 'might' be a virus. To do this you need to make sure you have installed some 'firewall' software. This is a program that constantly monitors your connection to the Internet and your email system. It blocks anything suspicious, including potential viruses. If you are not using a firewall program, you are laying yourself open to potential attack. No-one who uses email should run their system without a firewall in place.

Keeping messages secret

A valuable reason for having a firewall is that it can also protect your privacy. When your computer is connected to the Internet to retrieve your email, your entire machine is open to the world. Anyone, from anywhere, can take a peek; they can even extract data from your files. A firewall can prevent this from happening. However, it can also help ensure your confidential data stays away from prying eyes. For instance, your private email address can be detected when you are connected to the Internet. A firewall program can prevent this from happening, ensuring you retain a high degree of confidentiality.

> **Are you happy with anyone being able to see what your computer contains, where you have travelled on the Internet and to extract key information from your machine? When you collect your email and you are not protected by a firewall, all this is possible.**

Popular firewall programs include Norton Internet Security and McAfee Firewall. However, they are not enough on their own to provide complete security and confidentiality. You should also make sure you have a policy on security issues. Many businesses lose confidential data because of slipshod security measures. Staff can attach the wrong files to messages or send out data to the wrong email address. These errors can be avoided with proper internal security measures such as restricting access to certain files, or preventing particular kinds of data files from being attached.

> Do you know what security measures are in force for your computer system? It is worthwhile establishing a security policy and using the computers automation features to put it in place. If you don't have security measures in place on

your PC, it is worthwhile arranging them as soon as you can to protect confidential data.

Home users should also establish security measures. Many home PCs are shared and no matter how good your teenagers may be with the machine, there is every possibility they can let slip your home finances to someone. Equally, think how they would feel if you were able to access their directory of love letters! Security measures such as password protection and encryption of files will allow every member of the family to keep confidential matters personal.

> *"Until recently I had been receiving counselling for depression after my mother had died. I was encouraged to write a journal of my feelings each day as a form of therapy. I had hidden the files away in a folder that had a meaningless name. But I was horrified to discover that my daughter had been reading my notes. I dread to think what might have happened if she had decided to email them to her grandfather, my Dad."*
> Katherine A, mother.

Passwords can be applied to almost all files and folders on most PCs. However, some older computers might not be able to do this, so you'll need to install some additional software — that can be downloaded from the Web — to do this. However, passwords can be easily broken — you'd be amazed at the number of people who use their name or their initials as their password! So, to further enhance your security you may need to encrypt certain files. This means using a special program that re-writes your file in a special code. You decide who gets the decoding software and the password. Only those people who have both these items can unlock your data. Most email systems can incorporate encryption software so that you can encrypt files you send over the Internet. This means your email messages can be coded so that no-one, other than the intended recipient can decode them and read them. For sensitive information such encryption is essential, as the email network is an open system, meaning material flowing through it can be easily spied on. The most commonly used encryption software for email is called Pretty Good Privacy (PGP).

Do you send emails or files that you do not really want people to see, other than the intended recipient? If this is the case, you should consider adding encryption to your email system.

Using digital 'IDs'

A digital ID is an identification that helps prove your email is from you – and not from someone masquerading as you. You need to buy a digital ID from one of the suppliers, such as VeriSign, Global Sign, or Thawte. You need to provide some means of identifying yourself to the supplier, pay a fee and then you are sent your digital signature. You can install this within your email system so that each time you send out a message, your signature is attached. People receiving your email then have a way of being able to check you are who you say you are! Digital IDs are invaluable and really help you establish your identity in an email. Without them it is difficult to prove your status to unknown people. Many digital IDs also offer encryption facilities as well, so they have a dual purpose.

TIPS:

- ➤ Backup all your email files every day.
- ➤ Install anti-virus software and get it automatically updated.
- ➤ Add a firewall to your PC to protect you from hackers.
- ➤ Establish a security policy and make sure everyone understands it.
- ➤ Password-protect your sensitive files.
- ➤ Enhance your email program with encryption software.
- ➤ Get a digital ID to help prove your identity.

Chapter 5

Getting email anywhere

- ➢ Connecting from abroad
- ➢ Using web-based email
- ➢ Get email with your mobile
- ➢ Using auto responders

Connecting from abroad

> *"I was working in Spain for four weeks and had to dial my*
> *email service each day to get my messages. My phone bill*
> *was huge when I got home and I just wished I could have*
> *got my email from a local telephone connection."*
> Angus C, Account Director, public relations agency

The email service you subscribe to collects all your messages from
around the world and stores them on a computer called a 'mail server'.
When you connect to your email service you are dialling into this mail
server, so you are connecting to a specific computer and at a particular
location. So, if you need to access your email from abroad, you will
have to connect to that exact computer. This means if you use your
mobile your phone bills will be large as you'll be making international
roaming data calls to collect what might be large amounts of material.
Since you have no idea as to how big your messages may be, you have
no way of knowing how much data you will download. Consequently
when collecting your emails from abroad you face potentially large
mobile bills.

> Set your mobile to download just the 'header' information from your mail server. This prevents you from downloading attachments and large emails unless you need to. This will help minimise your mobile phone costs.

If you need to collect lots of email while abroad regularly, you may be better off using an Internet Café. This will avoid you needing to take your laptop around and will also mean you can save costs on your mobile phone.

> Do you travel abroad and would you like to collect your messages while away? Have you considered the costs of connecting to your email service?

If you are using your laptop abroad then make sure you log in to free Wi-Fi services wherever possible. Otherwise you will be tempted to use a mobile connection such as a tethered phone or a 3G adaptor, only to find that your data roaming bill is high.

> It's a good idea to have a 'travel kit' for collecting emails while abroad. This needs to contain your set of phone line adapters, plus your manual for your modem, and a list of telephone numbers for Internet access and for help lines.

Using web-based email

"I like checking my email when I'm abroad but I get frustrated at having to take my laptop so I can run the email program."
David K, Chairman, golf club

If you haven't already signed up for a web-based email

account as your 'public' address, it is a good idea to register for such a service as you'll be able to access your email from abroad.

Web-based email is commonplace and means you can access your messages no matter where you are; as long as you have web access you can check your emails. There are, of course, some difficulties with using web-based email. For a start, some of the web email companies limit the size of the files you send. This means you cannot send large attachments; hence you will suffer some limitations. Equally, it means other people cannot send you large files — or if they do, the email will be sent back to them ('bounced' back) as 'undeliverable'. Be sure to check the limitations of any webmail service you sign up for.

Also, some web-based email providers sometimes clear your old files out — so that they don't have to store vast amounts of messages. You should arrange for old files to be archived and sort them into folders but beware of any storage limits imposed by the email company – you don't want your email disappearing..!

If you do go abroad regularly on business, or want to catch up on important email while on holiday, you can get your normal email address diverted or copied to your web-based email address. Many ISPs allow you to perform this function yourself. Before you go away just set up the redirection and all your email will automatically get copied to your web-based inbox. You can then access this while away to keep up-to-date. On your return you just switch off the diversion and you are back to normal.

What would be the best approach to collecting email in your specific circumstances? Would the restrictions of web-based email and the administration you need to perform be acceptable?

If you do decide to use web-based email, you should make sure you have anti-virus and firewall software in place. In theory, it is easier for people to attack web-based email than that on traditional mail servers. Plus, since your email is only protected by a password — and not by a series of separate settings as in traditional email — your messages are much more vulnerable to attack. Therefore web-based email is not really suited to highly sensitive information. However, many webmail services do allow for "https" connections so make sure you always connect this way if possible.

Get email with your mobile

> *"The best thing I did to improve my email service was to buy a new mobile phone that had an integrated email application. The phone was a little more expensive than most mobiles, but it has transformed my work away from the office."*
> Peter B, Sales Executive.

> *"I have stopped taking my laptop abroad on business. I found I was only using it for emails and it seemed such an effort carrying all that weight just for my messages. I've bought a pad device and I get all me emails on that nowadays."*
> Mary D, Nutritionist, food processing company

The benefit of a mobile device for email – whether a phone or a tablet or pad devices - is that you can check your emails and stay in touch without having to lug around heavy laptops. Most people when abroad only use their laptops for email, so it makes sense to use a much lighter device if possible.

> How many messages are you likely to receive while
> away? If it is only a couple do you need to buy extra
> hardware such as a tablet or will your phone do? How
> long will these emails be? Asking yourself these
> questions before you set off on a trip could help you
> work out which kind of access you need while away.

If you are only going to receive a few short messages your mobile phone will be sufficient. Alternatively get a pad or tablet device if you wish to do more, such as the occasional document.

> Find out more about email on mobile phones by searching
> for 'unified messaging' on the Internet, or by going to the
> web site of your phone manufacturer.

Unified message services provide you with a single 'inbox' for email, voicemail and faxes. You can have them diverted to any number you like and some of the companies will convert emails into voice mail, or to SMS messages. Having a unified messaging service means you can improve your communication in business teams.

Using autoresponders

Sometimes you will not want to get your email from anywhere. Occasionally you will want the peace and quiet of being away from the hubbub of international communications. Every now and then, the solitude can be quite relaxing. For these reasons you may not want to connect to your email service. However, from the perspective of someone sending you a message, your lack of reply is either interpreted as rudeness or inefficiency. So you still need to reply to people who contact you. Luckily, you can do this without having to lift a finger while you are away from your desk. Most Internet Service Providers allow you to set up 'autoresponders'. These are messages that are automatically sent to everyone who sends you a message. Your messages will still be delivered to your inbox but everyone will have been sent a message 'by you' in the meantime. You can enter any text you like in these 'autoresponders' such as:

"I am away from my desk this week and will not be accessing my email. I will be in touch again next week when I get back from my trip abroad."

In this way your contacts are kept informed and you have only had to set this message up once, just prior to going away.

Autoresponders therefore help your professional image and also help your administration since you do not get additional, unwanted messages asking why you haven't replied to an earlier email. If you want to, you could get all your email redirected to your private inbox, so you can read it, but still have an autoresponder saying you are away. This means you can keep on top of things, but don't have to bother replying or doing any work until you are back at your computer.

TIPS:

➢ Set up email on your mobile properly to avoid costly roaming charges for large amounts of data.

➢ Get an account with an ISP abroad if you visit a particular country regularly.

➢ Set up a web-based email account so you can get email on any device.

➢ Consider buying a tablet or pad device to avoid lugging your laptop everywhere.

➢ See if you can upgrade your mobile phone to better receive email.

➢ Set up autoresponders to help administer your email while you are away.

Chapter 6

A complete email system

> ➢ Managing your email
> ➢ Sorting out your emails
> ➢ Avoiding spam
> ➢ Using auto responders

"Email takes up an average of one hour of my day – every day. That's a whole working day each week, roughly, spent just on email. I wish there was a better way of managing it."
Andrew B, Sales Manager, Hotel

Managing your email

If you don't manage email, then you are bound to waste time and have an impact on the productivity of you day. Why? Because even with the advent of social networking the amount of email is increasing. There are now around 250 billion email messages sent every day to 1.4 billion email users – that's around 180 messages every day of the week for each individual. And these numbers are predicted to more than double in the next three years. Like it or not, email is a significant part of our daily life and without management, it will become difficult to operate your business.

The first step in managing your email is to choose your system. There are three options:

> ➢ A dedicated email program, such as Microsoft Outlook or Thunderbird
> ➢ A webmail service, like Gmail or Hotmail
> ➢ A shared service combining web and desktop, like Microsoft Exchange

Most people appear to opt for a dedicated program using webmail as an alternative access or as a backup service. However, this often means you have to manually control the two systems – they are not completely connected and so there is a potential for conflict and errors.

There are some ways out of this conundrum, though. One is to use a synchronisation tool and keep your email system on a USB memory stick. You can then take it wherever you want, ensuring your email is always up to date with your backup file on your main PC. However, this assumes you always have access to a computer with a USB port. If you want email on your mobile, or you visit an Internet Café then this may not be practicable.

Is your current email system actually performing the way you want it to? Should you review it against the competition?

So, you need a system whereby your email can be "in sync" whether you are using your office computer, your laptop, your mobile phone, a computer in a client's office, a terminal at an Internet Café or an email program on a memory stick. There are a few options which enable you to do this (almost...!).

One is to use Microsoft Outlook on your PC and connect that with a Premiere Google Apps account (currently £33 a year). This allows you to ensure you have a virtual near-replica of your email system on your computer.

A similar system is Apple's MobileMe service, which lets you connect your desktop email program to an online system which also connects to your mobile devices.

An alternative is Zoho for Business which provides a host of features letting you share your settings and documents between your computer and "the cloud".

Also worth considering is the 1&1 MailXChange service. For individuals it costs less than £10 a month and provides a complete copy of your desktop system in a virtual, web-based access. The two remain in-sync and you are sure you will always have whatever you need, wherever you need it.

> Write a list of your email requirements covering all the
> features you need. Now check all the main email services
> to see which most closely matches your needs.

Of course, you can use free services, such as Gmail and Yahoo!
Mail to provide you with an online copy of your desktop email system.
However, that often requires lots of manual work, wasting time. Or you
end up with two systems that are never quite the same. Even if you use
the more sophisticated "IMAP" email system instead of the standard
"POP" system, things are never quite the same because any syncing of
old emails prior to setting up the webmail system has to be done
manually on both your desktop and your virtual system.

Whatever you do, the increased use of email and the more
mobile world we work in means you need to consider the system that
best works for you. Inevitably, you need a system that allows you
access old emails when you are away from your desk. Before you set
up any kind of management system, your first priority should be to
consider which methods of synchronisation you are going to use. One
good system is using Microsoft Outlook on a PC, together with a
Google Apps Premiere account for remote access and the Gmail App
on a smartphone. Together, they ensure that my email system is
replicated no matter where you are or what device you are using. An
alternative to this is to have an email account with your ISP which
copies all emails automatically to a webmail service such as Gmail.

Sorting out your emails

Once you have a synchronised system in place, the next thing to consider is how you are going to use it. The best way to use email is to take one of three decisions on incoming mail. You should either:

- ➤ Delete it
- ➤ Act on it
- ➤ Store it

There is little else you can do with emails. Yet, many people have inboxes which are crammed full of emails. All this does is to make it seem like you have more work than is the case – thus demotivating you. Furthermore, it makes it slow and difficult to find old emails which contain information you need. On top of that, it slows down your email system itself, further adding to the time wasted with processing emails.

> *"Every day when I open up my emails I am faced with an inbox that says there are more than 2,000 unread messages. It has been like this for months and most of the messages are ages old. I simply don't have the time to go through them all but the fact I can see so many need dealing with puts me off opening up my email program."*
> David S, Managing Director, Recruitment Company

The best thing to do is to set up an email system with multiple folders or directories. You could, for instance, have a folder for "Clients" and then sub-folders for each individual client. You might also have a folder for Newsletters and then sub-folders for each kind of newsletter, with further sub-divisions for each individual organisation that sends you newsletters.

You will end up with dozens of folders – but this makes things easier to find in the future. They are only storage folders – to hold emails that have been previously processed, or which contain information you do not currently need, but may require in the future.

When an email comes in all you need to do is decide whether it can be deleted straight away – that's easy. If it cannot be deleted consider whether you should answer it or deal with it in some way, or is it merely information you can use in the future?

If you can deal with it in about two minutes, do it now. If you cannot do that then it means the email should be marked for future use by putting it in an "Action" folder where you store emails for later work. Alternatively simply file it in the appropriate storage folder if you don't need to do anything more but need the information. This means your inbox is empty and you have an Action folder for dealing with later. When you have acted upon those emails, move them to the appropriate folder.

Avoiding spam

As mentioned earlier, you should have an efficient spam filter in place so that your inbox does not become cluttered with nonsense you have to manually move yourself. We spend about 10 minutes every day simply deleting spam. According to one study, this means filtering out spam appears to take up an entire working week out of your year. Another study even showed that around 10% of people have to spend 30 minutes every day, simply to delete spam from their inbox. Clearly, if you don't have a spam filter, any improved management of email is going to only have a partial impact. If you want to see some reviews and comparisons of spam filters, take a look at:

http://spam-filter-review.toptenreviews.com/

The complete email system

- ➤ Get two email addresses, one as your main address, the other for signing up to online services
- ➤ Get an email account with something like Gmail
- ➤ Divert your main address to Gmail by getting all incoming messages copied across
- ➤ Set up folders or labels in your webmail system, including an action folder
- ➤ Check your main address emails on your webmail system – so that you can check from anywhere on any device
- ➤ Check your other address occasionally directly at your email service provider just to ensure there are no important items in the inbox

TIPS

- ➤ Use a webmail service as your main email checking program so that you are always "in sync" no matter which device you connect with
- ➤ Set up folders or labels so that you can store your emails and find them easily
- ➤ Decide what to do with each email – delete, act or store
- ➤ Have an "Action" folder to put all emails which require replies that will take longer than two minutes
- ➤ Keep your anti-spam software up-to-date

Index

Y

Z

Graham Jones

Graham Jones can help you become effective and efficient using email. He runs three-hour workshops on effective email for businesses to help staff become more productive and avoid wasting time with their email system.

If you would like to get Graham to come and run a workshop at your premises please call: 0118 336 9710 or email graham@grahamjones.co.uk.